Champion:
Ten Ways to Develop A Successful Mindset

By

Paul G. Brodie

Champion: Ten Ways to Develop A Successful Mindset

Copyright @ 2017 by Paul G. Brodie

Editing by Devin Rene Mooneyham

All rights reserved in all media. No part of this book may be used or reproduced without written permission, except in the case of brief questions embodied in critical articles and reviews.

The moral right of Paul G. Brodie as the author of this work has been asserted by him in accordance with the Copyright, Designs, and Patents Act of 1988.

Published in the United States by BrodieEDU Publishing, 2017.

Disclaimer

The following viewpoints in this book are those of Paul Brodie. These views are based on his personal experience over the past forty-two years on the planet Earth, especially while living in the great state of Texas.

The intention of this book is to share his stories of both success and struggles with developing a successful mindset and what has worked for *him* through this journey.

All attempts have been made to verify the information provided by this publication. Neither the author nor the publisher assumes any responsibility for errors, omissions, or contrary interpretations of the subject matter herein.

This book is for entertainment purposes only. The views expressed are those of the author alone and should not be taken as expert instruction or commands. The reader is responsible for his or her future action. This book makes no guarantees of future success. However, by following the steps that are listed in this book the odds of increased success have a much higher probability.

Neither the author nor the publisher assumes any responsibility or liability on the behalf of the purchaser or reader of these materials.

The views expressed are based on his personal experiences within the corporate world, education, and everyday life.

This book is dedicated to my mom, Barbara "Mama" Brodie. Without her support and motivation (and incredible cooking) I would literally not be here today.

I am also dedicating this book to my coaching clients and the student authors (past graduates, present and future students) in my Book Publishing for Authors Implementation Program. You have all gone above and beyond chasing your dreams to become bestselling authors and I am proud to be able to help you accomplish your dreams.

Table of Contents

Free Training

Introduction

Free Audiobook

Chapter 1 Dealing with Adversity

Chapter 2 Make a Choice

Chapter 3 Be Coachable

Chapter 4 Gratitude and Humility

Chapter 5 Going All In

Chapter 6 Travel

Chapter 7 Having an Accountability Partner

Chapter 8 Expand Your Mind

Chapter 9 The Five Ones

Chapter 10 Work Hard AND Work Smart

Summary: The Journey of a Champion

Champion Seminar Invitation

More Books by Paul

About the Author

Acknowledgments

Contact Information

Quotes

Feedback

Free Training

Are you looking to write, publish and market your book to a #1 bestseller in the next 90 days?

I invite you to watch my Get Published Training.

If you are looking to write your own book on travel, business, self-help, or anything else related to non-fiction, this webinar is for you.

If you are writing fiction and children's books, this webinar is for you.

Entrepreneurs, the benefits of writing and publishing a book is an ideal way to build your business. Having a book will help you become an authority in your specific area of expertise.

This is what you will learn on this Free Online Workshop:

- How to turn your book into multiple revenue streams
- How to get your draft turned into an eye-catching book that will help increase sales and attract clients for your speaking, coaching, and online courses
- How to market your book including several promo companies that I will share on the training that are used for every book launch

WARNING: The Webinar is only available for a limited time.

Go to www.BrodieEDU.com and click on the Free Webinar tab to sign up today

Introduction

Welcome to Champion. My intention with this book is to help you develop a successful mindset. We will cover ten different ways that you can develop your successful mindset through a variety of techniques and concepts.

One of the biggest challenges in our lives is the ability to not only be positive, but to be positive on a *consistent* basis. There is a lot of negativity that we must consistently battle throughout our lives. I will provide you with the necessary tools to take charge and develop your successful mindset. In 2016, I created the Champion seminar with the intention of helping people shift their focus to the positive aspects of their lives to help them achieve their own success.

Chapter 1 Dealing with Adversity. I provide my own battle with dealing with adversity during the first part of 2017 and what I did to succeed.

Chapter 2 Making a choice. We cover the importance of creating an action plan and making the decision to change our mindset

Chapter 3 Be Coachable. We cover the importance of being coachable to help achieve our goals.

Chapter 4 Gratitude and Humility. Both are critical in developing a successful mindset.

Chapter 5 Going All In. In this chapter I share my transition to leaving teaching and successfully running both my companies and how you can do the same thing.

Chapter 6 Travel. This chapter is all about learning about yourself through the journey of travel and self-discovery.

Chapter 7 Having an Accountability Partner. We cover the importance of having someone to help keep you accountable whether that person is your friend, significant other, family member, or making the investment in hiring a coach.

Chapter 8 Expand Your Mind. We cover the importance of investing time each day to read to expand your mind. I also share multiple books that I personally recommend that will help you develop a successful mindset.

Chapter 9 The Five Ones. In this chapter I share the most effective way to become successful in business during the next year.

Chapter 10 Work Hard AND Work Smart. We cover not only the importance of hard work, but also working smart. I share ways that you can maximize each day to increase your own productivity significantly to help you succeed.

Summary: The Journey of a Champion. In the summary, we review the past ten chapters and go through next steps to help you become your greatest champion.

I hope this book helps you in your journey to develop your successful mindset. My philosophy in anything I do in life, whether it's teaching, giving motivational seminars, and writing and coaching, is to have the power of one. The power of one is my goal to help at least one person. I hope that person is you.

Free Audiobook

Are you a fan of audiobooks? I would like to offer you the free audiobook of Book Publishing for Authors ($15.00 Retail Price). All you need to do is go to my website at www.BrodieEDU.com/bpfa and provide your e mail address in exchange for the free digital download. The audiobook will only be available on the website for a limited time as I offer free goodies to my readership on a regular basis.

Chapter 1 Dealing with Adversity

"Everybody has a plan until they get hit in the face."
Mike Tyson

In life, we will all fall down at some point. There will always be setbacks. The question is what happens after you fall? Will you get up and rise or will you stay down?

One of my greatest challenges in life has been with weight. I was further reminded of this on January 11, 2017. It is a day that I will never forget. One of my students earned iPad time that day due to getting his work completed in class. The student was very familiar with the iPad and loves to take pictures with it.

I took the iPad back from the student and my assistant mentioned that I should probably check the iPad to see the pictures. Typically, I would delete the pictures to save space on the iPad at the end of the day. What I saw horrified me…

Within the many pictures the student took, he captured two horrible looking pictures of me. The student had a habit of using the zoom feature when he took pictures. He decided to zoom on my stomach. It was a picture of me holding the door for a student and all I saw was this big gut again.

The same big gut that I lost five years ago and thought I would never see again.

The second picture was of me sitting at my desk taking attendance. It was at the worse possible angle and again zoomed on my mid-section showing ample belly. I was so terrified after seeing the pictures that I contacted my doctor's office and set up an appointment that afternoon to get lab tests run and to get my slim shot again.

From November 2014 until June 2016 I took what was called a slim shot. The slim shot is an injection that helps you with both increased energy and metabolism and was a great help in losing weight, especially since losing weight is much tougher as you get older. The shot also had multiple vitamins including B12. I told my nurse I fell off the health wagon and needed their help. After arriving at the doctor's office for hormonal health I had to get weighed. I figured that I put on 10-15 pounds. I was wrong.

I had gained 31 pounds since June 2016. My weight was 320.1 pounds, only sixteen pounds less than that infamous day in May 2011 when I had my wake-up call, which I detail in my first book Eat Less and Move More (Kindle version is free for a limited time at www.BrodieEDU.com/books). It was time for wakeup call 1.0.

After getting my lab tests run and after the technician took three vials of blood to basically test everything, I spoke with the head nurse, who had helped me since starting the slim shots. She reminded me to avoid white and wheat flour at all costs and to also read every label to make sure I was not ingesting white or wheat flour.

Since I wrote my first book, Eat Less and Move More: My Journey (competed Summer 2015) my weight was pretty consistent going into June 2016. That was when the trouble started. In life, we tend to get a little soft and lose focus at times. June 2016, I was 289 pounds and on pace to make my weight goals. My sister was visiting for ten days and I wanted to show her the best of the Dallas/Fort Worth area and Austin. I also wanted to show her the best of the food in Texas.

That journey ballooned my weight to 297 pounds on my last weigh in on June 23. Over the previous months I noticed that my body built up a resistance to the slim shot that I took over the past year and a half. The slim shot helped with speeding up my metabolism and with providing additional vitamins. I figured I needed a break from the shot and could handle my food management while enjoying life a bit more. That was not the best idea.

After my sister left, I took my mom for an epic sixteen-day trip to Maui and wrote my sixth bestselling book about Maui while in Hawaii. It was an amazing trip and I knew that I gained some weight and was alright with that. The problem was that I was not that motivated to work out. I still did my work outs, but would only exercise three times instead of four. In addition, I had another trip two weeks later to Las Vegas to celebrate one of my oldest friend's 40th birthday. We went together on our first trip to Las Vegas back in 1998 and literally experienced our own version of The Hangover before it became a movie.

Las Vegas was a fun trip, but again I ate many different foods I should not have. In the past, after a vacation I would get a weigh in and then work my butt off for a week and take off any weight that I had gained. The problem was that I was feeling comfortable with life and I did not want to start the shot series and weigh ins again. This was a fatal error that I wrote about not making in my first book, yet I did it again.

After Vegas, I had a few more weeks off before the school year started. I kept consistent with my workouts and was feeling good about the new school year. I had a new teaching assignment in Fort Worth and loved working there with a great Principal and a wonderful group of fellow teachers. It felt like home. Again, I was content, happy, and didn't care that my clothes were a little tighter.

As the school year started I felt like I was losing weight. Some of my clothes felt a little looser and I was enjoying the start of the school year. As the fall semester progressed I started feeling worse and worse. After Christmas, I felt horrible and felt that something was wrong health wise after enjoying all of the holiday celebrations and rich foods.

My main mistake over the summer and fall of 2016 was eating sandwiches on a regular basis. Even though they were usually whole wheat or multigrain, with my age (41 at the time) my low thyroid level, combined with not weighing in at least twice a month, was a recipe for disaster.

On Thursday morning, January 12th, I was about to eat my usual protein bar. The same one I have eaten for breakfast for over three years. I decided to look at the label and the label said it had wheat flour in it. I took the protein bar back to the pantry and got an apple instead. I couldn't believe that the same protein bar I ate since 2014 had wheat flour in it. The one thing I must avoid when on the shot is wheat. It is amazing how easy it is to screw up a diet. I knew that I could not make any more mistakes.

Within five weeks after getting my act together I lost twenty pounds. My clothes were fitting looser and I felt great. It was tough getting back on track, but I felt much better going down the right path again. This time I was not going to settle for just weighing in the 290 range. I am 6 feet 3, with broad shoulders and the frame of a football and rugby player that can take on a lot of weight without looking terribly overweight. This time I was going to be my greatest champion and finish the job by getting to my previous weight by August 2017.

Throughout this book I will be detailing not only the weight loss, but also what we can all do to become our greatest champion with wellness, our mindset, and with our career to achieve a successful mindset.

Ask yourself the following questions:

How have you responded to setbacks in your life?

Are you willing to get up when you fall down?

Have you struggled with weight?

Chapter 2 Make a Choice

"I guess it comes down to a simple choice, really: Get busy living, or get busy dying." Andy Dufresne (as played by Tim Robbins in the Shawshank Redemption)

The above quote has been a recurring theme for many people including myself. We all have a choice in life and that is to be our greatest champion or our worst enemy.

I knew that I screwed up badly in January and was thankful for the wake-up call. With realizing my mistakes, I immediately created an action plan to not only live a healthier lifestyle permanently, but also a plan to not only lose weight, but to keep the weight off.

The first thing I had to do was to change my mindset. This had a profound effect as it changed my mindset in many ways. When I started to lose the weight once again I knew that it would be a long road ahead.

When you are forty-one years old, losing weight is much harder. The main thing I learned was that patience was going to be key.

Within five weeks after getting my act together I lost twenty pounds. My clothes were fitting looser and I felt great. It was tough getting back on track, but I felt much better going down the right path again.

What also changed was my mindset in many areas. One of the things I gave up was bread. My nurse mentioned that I most likely had a reaction to gluten and recommended that I give up bread and any food with wheat or white flour.

It was tough at first, but I noticed a huge difference in not only an increase in energy, but also with inflammation in my body. I had an old soccer injury that was bothering me throughout December and January and I figured the increase in weight was part of the problem with the inflammation.

I played intramurals in college and was the goalkeeper and coach of the soccer team. During one night game we were playing at Maverick Stadium at the University of Texas at Arlington, my alma mater. I got injured. The turf was old and was basically carpet.

It rained earlier that day and the turf was still wet. This is what caused an injury that I have had since that night in 2004. During the game, I was saving a shot on goal. The only problem is that I fell during the save. My body went one way and my left foot went the other.

I ended up stretching multiple ligaments on my left foot and this injury continues to flare up from time to time. It typically gets worse either when I gain weight or when I fly. The pressurized cabins on the plane in addition to the travel can cause inflammation. One thing I have learned this year is the benefit of compression socks as I have worn them on multiple flights. If you have this same issue, I highly recommend buying a pair because they help.

During that time, when I lost the first twenty pounds, I realized that I had a long road ahead. The weight came off quickly to start and I knew the rapid weight loss would slow down and it did. I decided to make another change as March approached and took a risk to improve my energy further.

In March, I had a procedure done to increase testosterone. When you hit your late thirties and forties as a man, it's common to have lower testosterone levels. My testosterone was low and I decided to have a procedure done to help increase my energy and continue to improve my health.

My doctor's office specializes in help with wellness and with BioTE and Slim Shots. BioTE is essentially help with hormones for men and women. After having my labs tested in January, I found that I had very low testosterone. The average level in guys my age is supposed to be over 1000 and I was hovering over 100. Therefore, as you can see, there was a huge discrepancy.

They offered a procedure where they implant testosterone pellets above your butt cheek. They even let you choose which cheek! The procedure costs $320.00-$370.00 depending on the dosage. Due to my size and my low testosterone level I had the higher dose.

The cost of the procedure was half price by going to a training event. The event is where new medical providers learn how to do the procedure and the patients serve as the test subjects so to speak. I say this because the people in the room who are learning how to do the procedure, are led by a nurse who has done the procedure many times and is very good at their job.

If you are squeamish at all, please skip the next paragraph.

They have you lay on your side and then numb the area where they make the incision. That is the easy part. Then the hard part begins. They insert the testosterone pellets into a metal rod device in a clockwise position until each pellet is installed. Usually the number of pellets range from six to eight. Each pellet must be properly inserted underneath the skin. They typically have three people who are part of the procedure with the nurse and take turns implanting the pellets in you. Unfortunately, one of the people had no idea what she was doing and after several attempts finally got the pellets installed. Due to this I ended up having a longer and more painful recovery time.

For those who skipped the paragraph, welcome back.

The recovery time is usually a week and my recovery took two weeks due to all the bruising. I mention this because I have no regrets. The procedure did help me long-term, but I always want to make clear that you do take certain risks with any procedure.

Once the procedure is completed, which takes twenty to thirty minutes on average, they put on an ice pack to the area and you are done. The stitches are steri-strips (or butterfly stitches) and will dissolve within a week. You will need five to seven days to recover due to swelling in the area. I will be completely honest; the first procedure is usually the roughest. I had bruising for three weeks and it took eight days to recover. Ice will be your best friend during the recovery process.

I felt a difference within two weeks. I had increased energy and felt much better, even after injuring my knee at school. It was a tough decision, but I am glad I took the risk because it did improve my overall health.

The procedure was done during spring break and I was off that week. At the time, I was still wrestling with the decision whether to continue teaching.

On March 20, I was back at school after spring break. Within an hour of being back at school I suffered my first injury as a teacher. As a Special Education Teacher working directly with special needs kids on a daily basis, meltdowns do happen. It is important to note that one of my students had concerning behavior prior to spring break.

When teaching Special Education, you get used to the occasional meltdown, and have training to deal with those situations. I have been very fortunate that within a little over three years I have never gotten hurt and neither have my kids. Usually, when you see concerning behavior with a special needs student prior to a holiday break, they typically return with much better behavior, at least for a few weeks.

I figured with this student, a week home would help him and he would be rested and ready for a few productive weeks before the state testing started. I was wrong!

Within one minute of being in my classroom, the student had a meltdown. I kneeled on the ground with my right knee on the carpet. This was to keep proximity with the student and to stay at eye level as he was kneeling on the floor, where he usually does when having a meltdown.

He started to calm down, but then got up quickly, ran across the room and grabbed a chair in an attempt to hit another student with the chair. The student had already tried to hit another student with a chair on several occasions throughout the year. I got up immediately to help the student calm down and heard a loud pop in my knee and ripped my pants at the right knee.

After calming down the student, I notified my school administration what happened and requested permission to stay at school with my pants ripped. I did not want to drive twenty miles home just to change pants. They were fine with me staying. They knew I was needed in the classroom to help the kids.

Things like this do happen and I have heard horror stories about injuries to Special Education Teachers from broken arms and legs to teachers who had to get knee replacements. I never took it personally when a student had a meltdown because I knew they would never intend to hurt anyone. The student wanted their own way and some kids do communicate through violence.

My mentality was to move on and get through the day. At the time, I felt a twinge in my knee and figured it would go away. It got worse! On Tuesday, I started to feel a throbbing pain. On Wednesday, when I sat down in a booth at a restaurant I felt like someone stabbed me in my right knee and I screamed in pain. At that point, I knew something was wrong.

I toughed it out on Thursday, but on Friday decided since the pain was getting worse that I would have to report it to my administration.

They already knew of the incident so at least it would not be a surprise.

After reporting the injury and filling out the paperwork, I had an appointment at CareNow that afternoon. The Doctor was not able to diagnose what was wrong and she referred me to a specialist to get an MRI of my knee. She saw the amount of pain I was in and knew an MRI was the only way to see the injury properly as the X-rays were not clear.

On Monday, I had to go to human resources to meet about my injury and bring my paperwork from CareNow. The doctor had me on multiple restrictions due to my right knee including no lifting, no pushing, no pulling, no escorting, limited movement, no walking upstairs, etc. Due to the incident and the school not able to accommodate my restrictions I was put on assault leave for a few days until they could figure out a plan. I was off on Monday and Tuesday and returned on Wednesday.

On Wednesday, I had my MRI and got the results on Friday. My meniscus not only had damage, but I was also diagnosed with arthritis on my knee. Due to the injury, I had updates to my restrictions and had to go back to HR with the updated restrictions the following Monday.

During that week, we had several meltdowns by the student including one incident where he threw a chair over five feet. I requested that a camera be added inside my classroom due to safety concerns and that I didn't feel safe, especially with having limitations with my knee. The student was reassigned to my teacher assistant due to the assault and he knew that I was no longer dealing with him directly and knew that he could get away with additional bad behavior.

During this time, I had two additional weigh-ins. On March 22, I weighed in at 301.0 and on March 29 was 302.0. It was incredibly frustrating putting on the weight. My nurse did mention that I would most likely have water retention from the pellets for a few weeks and the stress of my school situation was also most likely a factor. I was still eating clean and had no cheat meals, but the pellets plus the stress lead to a weight gain and I was over 300 once again.

I also ended up been put on leave once again for a week after meeting with human resources. With the additional restrictions one of the things put in place was to have a second assistant in my classroom as I would most likely be on restrictions for the remainder of the school year.

The school was not able to get a second assistant for a week so I was not able to work. Due to my concerns about safety and the risk about further injury, I did not mind being docked a few days' pay if it meant not risking further injury.

On March 31, the Principal found someone to help as a long-term sub for the rest of the school year and I was back at work on April 3. I did meet with HR that morning with my union representative to get certain assurances in case the sub was absent.

Serving as a teacher is tough and teaching with a huge knee brace and having limited mobility in a special needs classroom can be quite daunting. During this time, I realized that I needed to make a choice and get busy living. That choice was that it was finally time to leave teaching. The injury was not the primary reason, but getting hurt did make my decision easier as I did not want to end up having to get knee replacements and potentially getting other injuries.

Life will serve you a lot of curveballs. What you must realize is that you must choose what to do when you get the curveballs. You can act like a victim or you can see it as an opportunity. I chose to see everything as an opportunity and took action to get busy living.

During this time, I had the biggest curveball yet. Once you have your first testosterone procedure done you do get additional lab tests a few weeks later. After my labs were taken my testosterone levels skyrocketed, but then I got the next curveball.

My nurse then mentioned that one of my levels came back elevated and she was concerned as this area was not tested previously. She wanted me to get a CT (Cat) scan done as soon as possible. I asked why and she said there was a good possibility that I had a growth on my pituitary gland and if so then there was a chance that it could be cancer.

Ask yourself the following questions:

Are you at a fork in the road where you need to make a life changing decision?

Have you ever had a health scare?

When adversity strikes do you feel like a victim or do you see it as another opportunity to rise?

Chapter 3 Be Coachable

"The journey of a thousand miles begins with one step." Lao Tzu

Cancer is a listed as a six-letter word, but I refer to it as a four-letter word, and the word repulses me. I lost my aunt Jackie to brain cancer when I was young and her daughter (my cousin Alison) died of pancreatic cancer in 2013 when Alison was fifty years old. There are two things that are prevalent on both sides of my family: cancer and depression. Both suck!

The idea that I may have cancer was terrifying. I have always been a believer that things come in threes. Throughout my life big events always came in three as did scary events. In January, two things happened...

First, the weight gain that I immediately took control over. The second, a high-speed collision that happened at the end of January. I was driving home from school after teaching for the day. The commute was only twenty minutes and mainly involved driving on the freeway home. I was driving in the fast lane and due to the speed of traffic was doing sixty miles per hour. There was a red truck that was behind me and then illegally went into the shoulder of the freeway and then went into my lane and hit my SUV.

I could not believe the person hit me. It was scary being hit while going that fast. Immediately, I went into the other lane and fortunately, there was not a car in the lane. The guy then shook his fist at me and sped away. I then chased him down as I was not going to let him get away with a hit and run.

I calmly called 911 to report the incident and told them his license plate and that it was a hit and run. They told me to go to the police station to report the incident, which I did. The police tracked him down later that evening and he did admit to hitting me and claimed that he didn't see me nor realized what happened.

My main thoughts during that time were of gratitude as it could have been much worse. Fortunately, I was in a great SUV that protected me and the damage was not too bad. I was mainly shaken up, but realized that I was very lucky.

The most surreal part was driving to work the next morning. I was nervous at first to drive again, but got over it quickly. As I drove to work, there was a bad car wreck on the other side of the freeway almost exactly where my accident occurred. There were two cars flipped over and one of them looked identical to the red truck that hit me. The police officer did mention the man that hit me was already involved in multiple accidents, all his fault. I felt very lucky with what happened as I knew that things can always be worse.

When the nurse told me about the possibility of cancer in my brain, it really put things into perspective. The first thing I realized was that I would have to lie to my mom, out of necessity. I hate lying! It is one of my biggest pet peeves and I take great pride in being honest and blunt (at times to a fault).

My mom was turning eighty at the time and had high blood pressure in addition to type 2 diabetes. She is also a very protective mama and I knew the stress could cause her to have a stroke. With that in mind I only told a couple people. One was one of my best friends who kindly met me at the radiology location where I was to have my CT. There was an issue at the location and they refused to honor my appointment.

After speaking with the manager, they referred me to Baylor medical and Symeon went with me to the location and I had the CT done (shout out to

Symeon Melikoglou). It was scary not only with the CT and going into that narrow cylinder they put you in, but also the loud noises the machine makes. They also put in IV into you and was the first time I have ever had one. They put some warm fluid mixture in the IV before the scan and it took every bit of nerve to not get sick, but I sucked it up and got through it. Twenty minutes later it was done and I was on my way home.

Within twenty-four hours I had the results and had to go to my doctor's office to get the information. After arriving my nurse told me that I had a clean bill of health and that my brain was in great shape, especially for someone my age. The feeling of elation was incredible and the next step was to tell my mom the truth. She was not happy at me to say the least, but understood why I did it.

It was a scary time and a strange start to the first three months of the year. What I learned was to be coachable. When my nurse suggested the scan I immediately got it, even though it cost me sixteen hundred dollars. I did not want to live with the possibility that I had cancer, especially after I have already lost several members of my family.

It was during this time that I gave serious consideration to my future and decided that making a change in my life was my top priority. I picked up a book during this time and it was life changing. It was called Million Dollar Coach.

I got the book for Kindle back in December 2016 and as many people do, put it on the back burner. With everything that was going on I decided to finally start to read the book. It was lifechanging.

Million Dollar Coach was written by Taki Moore. Taki is a multi-millionaire who coaches other coaches and is the real deal. I ended up reading his book three times, something I have never done with a book.

During that time, I was very busy with teaching and with running both BrodieEDU and Brodie Consulting Group and I budgeted thirty minutes of time to read one chapter each day. Reading the book made me realize (as I hope this book does for you) that I can leave my present job and focus on my businesses and have great success and you can do the same.

I followed Taki's framework and structure and came up with a plan to be able to scale my coaching. What I realized is that my coaching was too broad and that I needed to focus on just one area. That area was book publishing as most of my clients were from that area.

With writing, publishing, and launching my books, I became very good at the process and created a book publishing system that launched all my books to a #1 bestseller and all of my clients. The problem was that one-on-one coaching was taking up too much time out of my schedule. I needed to change to a group coaching model so that I could scale my business.

Being honest, most people want to do everything their way. It does not work! I had to learn that the hard way and after realizing that I knew I needed to be more coachable to accomplish my dreams and goals. It was one of the best decisions I have ever made.

During this time, I made the decision to leave teaching. The knee injury was yet another wake-up call that it was time to make a change. While I love my kids, and had an amazing assistant, school, and Principal, it was time to make a choice and leave teaching once and for all.

My weight was much better and I was under three hundred and never weighed that much since. The testosterone implants did increase my energy and helped me gain muscle. My clothes were fitting looser and I gained additional notches on my belt.

Ask yourself the following questions:

Have you decided to make a huge career change before, if so how did you feel?

Have you taken the plunge and decided to change your life for the better?

Chapter 4 Gratitude and Humility

"Gratitude is the healthiest of all human emotions. The more you express gratitude for what you have, the more likely you will have even more to express gratitude for."
Zig Ziglar

With making the decision to finally leave teaching I set up a meeting with both my Principal and Vice Principal. The first thing I did was thank them both for their support with the injury and for their support throughout the school year.

They were both disappointed, especially the Vice Principal. My Principal was leaving the school at the end of the school year too. She is one of the best Principals I have worked with and I made it clear that this decision was in the making for a long time.

When I interviewed for the position the previous year, I did make clear that teaching was going to be a year-to-year decision and she was fine with that and appreciated my honesty. As I mentioned in PMA, she hired me on site and I did enjoy my final year of teaching in Fort Worth overall.

The classroom was amazing and she was great about making sure I had enough resources for my program. The main feeling I had for my final two months of teaching was gratitude.

This was also a transition time as I knew that I needed to get started with revamping my coaching program and decided to join Taki's Million Dollar Coaching Implementation Program. It was a ten-week program with live group coaching calls every two weeks in a group setting and weekly video modules that you received every week.

I was so impressed with the program and knowledge that I used the framework (with Taki's approval) of the program to create the Book Publishing for Authors Implementation Program. The program has five live group coaching calls and ten video modules (including two bonus modules). Now, all I had to do was unpack my Intellectual Property (IP).

This whole process was quite humbling as I was always the one to create programs and lead the way. I was still doing that, but under the guidance of an amazing coach with his framework.

When you have a great coach that you trust and respect, the best thing to do to paraphrase Kendrick Lamar, is to sit down and be humble. I sat at the learning tree and absorbed as much information about unpacking our IP and learning about frameworks and processes.

Fortunately, I had a ton of knowledge about book publishing, especially what works and what doesn't. I was ready to unpack this knowledge and get started the moment that my teaching career ended in early June.

The final two months of my teaching career were great. My Principal as part of my restrictions hired a long-term substitute, for the rest of the school year. The sub was fantastic and worked great with the kids. I was also going through physical therapy to rehab my knee.

It took time, but by the end of the school year my knee was healing and by the end of my final day at school (the day after the kids go home for the summer) I no longer had to wear my knee brace. The last week of school was emotional. Throughout the previous two weeks I took down several items a day in my classroom and took them home to put in storage. That way it was much quicker to take all my stuff from the classroom without doing everything at the last minute.

Each item reminded me of great memories throughout my teaching career with students who created custom Mr. Brodie poster designs for me to instructional items that I used to teach my kids. The toughest item to take down was the picture area next to my desk where I had pictures of friends, family, and students that were collected over the past nine years. It was great to go down memory lane and reminded me of the impact that good teachers have on their kids.

We also had a year-end party for the kids. It was during the party when I planned to tell the parents that I was not returning.

During the party, I thanked all the parents for their support with their kids throughout the school year. I had seen great improvement in the kids with the structure, discipline, and instruction and was very proud of them. The support of parents is critical to the success of the classroom and I thanked them for being great tag team partners throughout the year. Then, I started to get a lump in my throat.

I told them that this year was my final year in teaching and I thanked each of them for all their support. During this time, I also made it clear that I was leaving teaching and not teaching anywhere else and made it clear that it was a pleasure and honor to teach their children. All the parents immediately stood up and gave me a huge round of applause and thanked me for everything I have done to help their child.

The lump in my throat increased and I could barely get a word in without tearing up as I was unprepared for their response. It was incredibly humbling and a great honor for them to give me the kind ovation. The feeling I felt was like in those movies about teaching like Mr. Holland's Opus, or Freedom Writers. It brought my teaching career full circle and reminded me of the impact that good teachers can have on students and their families.

The day after the kids went home for summer, the teachers had their final work day. My mom has asked me all year if she could see my classroom and I agreed to take her with me for the final day. I asked my principal in advance if that was alright and she approved my request.

I arrived that final morning and I felt closure on my nine-year teaching career. There was no doubt in my mind that it was the correct decision. Mom got to meet my Principal, Vice Principal, and many of the teachers (including my amazing teacher assistant) that I referred to as not only colleagues, but also friends.

It was the ideal way to end a nine-year career and that chapter of my life was now finished. My health was getting better every day and my weight was in the high 280's down from over 320 in January. Now it was time to begin the next chapter and go all in.

Ask yourself the following questions:

When changes happen in life do you feel gratitude?

Do you find it difficult to be humble and learn from others?

Chapter 5 Going All In

"Life, like poker has an element of risk. It shouldn't be avoided. It should be faced." Edward Norton

When playing poker, the term all in refers to when someone risks all their chips on a hand. If they win they will make a lot of money and if they lose then the game is over for them. With leaving teaching in June, I was now all in.

I had a significant amount of money that I put together to get the business going. It was a transition to change from the one-to-one coaching model to the one to many group coaching model, but it was working. I had my first webinar in mid-June and afterwards had my first group of students join the Book Publishing for Authors Implementation Program. Now it was time to get going.

I had the Intellectual Property in my head and now it was time to deliver the content. Each week I created a slide show of that area of book publishing ranging from finishing your draft to my book publishing system to help market their book to a #1 bestseller. I had a great time building the content and it was hard work.

You will never work harder then you will when working for yourself. Eighty hour work weeks were common and I loved it. Once the slide show was completed I would record and narrate the module. I had such a great time recording the module with expanding on each slide and sharing my philosophy on publishing and helping my student authors with their books.

Ten weeks later my first group of students were through the program and they loved the course. One week later my second group of student authors went through the program and they raved about how much it has helped them.

The best part is helping my students. One of my current students has spent forty years writing her first book and now she has finished the book thanks to the program. I get to continue to serve as an educator, just in a different way. Best part is that I get to see my student authors grow and evolve in the program each week and it feels almost identical to helping my kids for the past nine years. The biggest takeaway is that everyone learns differently and good teachers find a way to teach all their students.

Seeing my students succeed is my greatest joy about the program. It has been life changing to them and to me. Getting to be your own boss is an amazing feeling. My commute is ten seconds from the living room to my home office and I am hoping to help as many students as possible become #1 bestselling authors and help change their lives so they can do the same.

Going all in can be a scary thing because you no longer have a monthly check arriving. You must live on the income you bring in. That is why I put enough money together to survive for eight months with no income just in case. Fortunately, revenue started to come in during the first month and we have grown every month since. We started to have five figure months and I have never looked back on the decision to leave teaching with any regret.

My health was even better and my weight was down to the low 280's. The commitment to stop eating bread, wheat and white flour, and limiting sugar made all the difference. I was working harder than ever, but my stress level was low and I love being my own boss.

The best part is the freedom to do what you want when you want to. I am writing this book while in Kihei, Hawaii otherwise known as my home away from home. This is something I never could have done when teaching with spending the second half of October in Maui. Getting away at times is critical and in the next chapter we will cover the importance of traveling.

Ask yourself the following questions:

Have you risked it all by going all in to build your own business?

Does the idea of leaving your current job scare or excite you?

What are you willing to invest to change your life?

What is it costing you currently to not change your life?

Chapter 6 Travel

"To travel is to take a journey into yourself." Danny Kaye

I love to travel! One of the greatest lessons I learned about myself was when I was twenty-years old. I decided for my twenty-first birthday that I wanted to travel to England and Scotland by myself. I had family in both countries and all I needed was a plane ticket and I was good to go.

It was an amazing journey as I was scared and homesick at first. The journey taught me self-reliance and I learned more about myself in that twenty-three days traveling through England and Scotland than I ever knew before. I returned to Texas the day before my twenty-first birthday a different and evolved person. The journey was life-changing and was a great gift.

In October 2017, I ended up spending more time out of Texas than in it. Started the month by flying to Los Angeles, California for two days. I was meeting with my business coach at his workshop in Santa Monica on October 2. On October 1st, I got to explore, which is the best thing about traveling.

I am part extrovert and part introvert. October 1st was a prime example when I met several friends for brunch (shout out to Whitney Massey, Charlie Kenney, and Zenon Acosta) at an awesome restaurant called Good Stuff in Hermosa Beach. We had a great time and enjoyed amazing food. I have always felt the best way to bring people together is great food and this was a prime example. Whitney lives in the Los Angeles area and both Charlie and Zenon ironically are from the area where I live in Texas and were on vacation that weekend in Los Angeles.

After brunch, I decided to explore Hermosa Beach, Venice Beach, and the Santa Monica Pier. I loved hanging out with my friends, but I also enjoy exploring new areas by myself. One of the greatest lessons we can learn is by spending time with ourselves.

Spending time with yourself can be counterintuitive if you do not like who you are. I had a great time exploring Hermosa Beach, Venice Beach, and the Santa Monica Pier. The beaches were amazing and the weather was perfect. Sunset at the Santa Monica Pier is a must if you are ever in the area. It was a great start to the trip.

One week later I was presenting my Motivation 101 seminar in Myrtle Beach, South Carolina. The day before the seminar my friend Ollie and I went to a great restaurant called the Calabash Seafood Buffet for amazing seafood (shout out to Ollie Moses). Afterwards Ollie had to take care of some work issues and I asked him to drop me off at Myrtle Beach. With being both an extrovert and introvert, I feel it is a great balance while you can both enjoy the company of friends, but also enjoy time by yourself. I feel this balance is critical in our own growth and development. To be able to love and care about others you must also love and care about yourself and this is a great way to do so.

The following day we had an amazing seminar for Motivation 101 with a great crowd. After the seminar, I stuck around to watch my friend Darrick give his seminar and had a great time (shout out to Darrick Williams). Typically, I escape to my hotel room after a seminar as I am usually physically and mentally spent. One of the things about having the introvert side is that I need to have time by myself (introvert time) after spending time in a social setting for a while. After the seminar and lunch, I went to my hotel room to take a little break to decompress and then went back down to enjoy the rest of the conference.

After getting back home for a week it was time for Maui. In 2016, when in Maui, I wrote my first travel book and it became a big success. For this trip, I brought several copies to give away to the businesses that we frequented as a thank you.

It was a cool feeling to be able to give these businesses a token of my appreciation and thank them for the great food and items. Best part was that several of them already knew about the book as travelers brought the paperback version of Maui with them on their trip.

If you love travel, then I highly recommend writing your own travel book. The process is very easy if you enjoy writing. Several of my student authors are writing books about travel including one of my students that lives in Kihei. I got to meet my student who lives in Kihei during the trip and gave her a copy of my Maui book as a gift. It was an amazing feeling to meet one of my student authors in person and tell her how proud I am of her progress and journey.

The greatest advice I can give you whether it is writing or running another business is to do what you love. If I was still teaching there would be no way that I could be in Maui and writing this book. The trips to Los Angeles and Myrtle Beach would also most likely never happened as I would be either teaching or preparing lesson plans for my kids.

Having the freedom to do what you want when you want is the greatest feeling you can have as a business owner. It can be stressful at times and it is hard work, but at the end of the day you are working for yourself. You also have one person to be accountable to and that is yourself. I did add an additional layer of accountability, which I will cover in the next chapter.

Ask yourself the following questions:

Do you like to travel?

Would you like to have the freedom to travel whenever you wanted to?

Would you like to have a job where all you need is a laptop and wireless internet connection?

Chapter 7 Having an Accountability Partner

"Great leaders understand that talented people thrive in a culture where accountability is a support system for success." Daniel Pink

One of the greatest pieces of advice I can give you is to have an accountability partner. An accountability partner can be a family member, friend, significant other, mentor, or a coach. I am a big believer in having a coach. I not only coach others, but I also have my own coach.

On October 2, I took the next step and joined Taki's Black Belt Mastermind program. I saw the benefit that his first course had on my career and I had no hesitation in signing up for Black Belt. The investment was significant, but the most important lesson I have learned this year is the power of investing in yourself.

Instead of looking at the cost of a program you must look at the outcome. Focusing on the outcome changed my mindset and caused me to look at things differently. Since I already had a significant return of investment on Taki's first course I had no fear of making the investment of joining Black Belt.

There are three key things you want to have in an accountability coach. You want someone who will help you with focus, accountability, and implementation. Those three areas are critical. Coaches like myself and Taki freely give away our information. What we charge a premium for is the implementation part as that is the most critical element of being successful.

One thing I want to make clear is that no one can do it themselves. We all need help! I am a huge believer in having help. It was the best decision I ever made with hiring my coach and going through his program. The money I invested in the program was significant, but I have already made significant revenue due to what I learned in his program. It was life changing when I decided to hire a coach to help me implement. Best part is that the investment often is tax deductible. Check with your country's tax laws, but I was able to write off the investment of hiring my own coach on my taxes.

I mention this because having the right mentality is key when you are ready to make serious changes and improvement in your life. The main thing to look for is what will the outcome be? I already know that my outcome with the return on investment will be significant because of the focus, accountability, and implementation that comes with Taki's Black Belt program.

Having a coach brings focus, accountability, and implementation. It also will help build your business quickly with a proven system that works. The hardest part about building any business is the implementation process, which is the primary benefit you will get when hiring a coach.

Ask yourself the following questions:

Do you believe in having an accountability partner?

Are you willing to invest in hiring someone to help you?

What are you willing to invest to change your life?

Chapter 8 Expand Your Mind

"I fear not the man who has practiced 10,000 kicks once, but I fear the man who had practiced one kick 10,000 times." Bruce Lee

Expanding your mind is key. I love to learn and reading books is one of the best ways to do so. We are all busy, but I challenge you to read for thirty minutes a day. It will not be easy at first, but once you schedule time to read daily, you will be amazed by how much you can read.

These are a list of my favorite books in addition to Million Dollar Coach, which you can get on Amazon. Most of the books I mention are available in Kindle, Paperback, and audiobook versions. I am old school and prefer the paperback versions. I highly recommend checking them out if you are looking to add books to your collection.

Recommended Books (Go to www.half.com to get most of the recommended books for under $5.00 each including shipping)

Success Through a Positive Mental Attitude by Napoleon Hill and W. Clement Stone

How Full Is Your Bucket by Tom Rath

The Last Lecture by Randy Pausch

Teach with Your Heart: Lessons I Learned from The Freedom Writers by Erin Gruwell

The Art of War by Sun Tsu

Steve Jobs by Walter Isaacson

Moneyball: The Art of Winning an Unfair Game by Michael Lewis

Total Recall: My Unbelievably True Life Story by Arnold Schwarzenegger

Tao of Jeet Kune Do by Bruce Lee

Tuesdays With Morrie by Mitch Albom

The Last Lecture is one of my all-time favorite books. Randy Pausch was diagnosed with pancreatic cancer and wanted to give what he called his last lecture at the university where he taught. His lecture was amazing and you can access it on YouTube. He discusses his philosophy on life and it was an incredible event. Randy passed away due to pancreatic cancer, but his legacy lives on.

Tuesdays With Morrie by Mitch Albom is another of my favorites. Mitch shares the story of reconnecting with his favorite college professor who was diagnosed with ALS, Lou Gehrig's

Disease. They would meet on Tuesday's and Morrie would share lessons about what he has learned over his life. This one hit close to home as I had a college professor named Dr. James Crosby who had a similar impact on my life. Morrie also reminded me of my grandfather as I had many chats with my granddad when I spent time with him. He passed away in 2003 and there is not a day that goes by that I do not think about him.

Teach with Your Heart by Erin Gruwell is the ideal book for teachers or for those who want to go into teaching. The movie, Freedom Writers is Erin's story about becoming a first-year teacher and the incredible impact she had on her students. It was the book and movie that inspired me during my first year of teaching as I have taught elements of the freedom writers method throughout my teaching career.

Total Recall by Arnold Schwarzenegger is one of the ultimate rags to riches story. The book will really surprise you as Arnold is not only quite the character, but also a highly successful businessman and was already a millionaire before he went into acting. The stories he tells are wildly entertaining and I literally could not put down the book as I read it over several days.

Tao of Jeet Kune Do by Bruce Lee is the final book I will cover. If you are looking to truly change your mindset then read about Bruce Lee's philosophy on life. The quote that had the most impact on me was about perfecting your life and mindset, which I shared at the start of this chapter. "I fear not the man who has practiced 10,000 kicks once, but I fear the man who had practiced one kick 10,000 times." Bruce Lee

That is the prime example of perfecting your business. The principal I believe in most about building a business is implementing the five ones, which we will cover in the next chapter.

Ask yourself the following questions:

Do you enjoy reading?

Are you willing to invest thirty minutes a day to expand your mind?

What is your favorite book?

Chapter 9 The Five Ones

"It is those who concentrate on but one thing at a time who advance in this world." Gary Keller

When I learned about the five ones from Taki earlier this year it was lifechanging. One of the biggest mistakes we make running our businesses is not focusing on the main thing. The five ones teach you how to focus on the one main thing that is going to make your business successful within the next year.

There are five parts to the five ones.

1. One Person! Who is that one person in regards to your target market? Who are the people you want to help? My target market is men and women 25-64 who are working full-time for the man and are wanting to write their book to build their business and full-time business owners who want to increase their authority (root word is author) in their area of expertise and increase their brand and revenue.
2. One product! What product do you want to sell? You want to sell one product to your one target market. My product is the Book Publishing for Authors Implementation

Program where I help people write, publish and market their book to a #1 bestseller in the next 90 days.

You need for your product to be amazing. The Book Publishing for Authors Implementation Program in my view is amazing. It includes ten video modules covering the entire book publishing process from finishing your book, finding the best book cover, how to get reviews, my entire book marketing system and is the same exact system that I have used to launch all my books to bestselling status as a #1 bestseller and also all of my clients, how to maximize revenue streams on the front-end with how to have your book available in Kindle, Paperback, and Audiobook formats for your launch (including how-to guides), how to build your audience, how to offer back-end products to maximize revenue from public speaking, online courses, and coaching.

In the program, we take a deep dive into each area of book publishing and the weekly modules average between thirty-five to fifty-five minutes for each module. The modules are sent out on a weekly basis for ten weeks and you also get two bonus modules including several additional bonuses from joining our Book Publishing for Authors secret Facebook group, free gifts including an autographed paperback copy of my #1 bestseller Book Publishing for Authors, a free sixty minute One-On-One strategy session with me and several other bonuses. With the program, the most important part is that it isn't done for you or do it yourself. It is done with you as we implement together and that is the secret sauce when you choose to work with me.

3. One conversion tool! What conversion tool will you use to sell your product? My main offer is my Book Publishing for Authors Implementation Program. The program is offered at the end of my free Get Published Webinar Training. In the webinar, I teach a lot of great content that helps people publish and market their book regardless of whether they decide to join my program.

I have always believed in offering the best content possible and in the training, we teach amazing content for the first forty-five minutes. In the final fifteen minutes, I go over the offer as we do offer a significant discount for anyone who joins the program during the webinar.

4. Lead Channel! What method of traffic will you use for marketing? You have three different channels to choose from.

The first channel is joint ventures where you will team up with someone to sell your product. You will most likely split the revenue with your JV partner fifty/fifty.

The second channel is paid ads, otherwise known as Facebook advertising. You do pay for the advertising, but you get to keep all the money that you made after advertising costs. It can be expensive and you do have to do a lot of testing. What I ended up doing was hiring an advertising agency that specializes in running Facebook ads. The startup cost can be several thousand dollars, but the return when done correctly will make you back potentially five to ten times that amount monthly.

Third channel is by using your email list to promote your product. Hopefully you have built up an email list between several hundred to several thousand people. It costs money to build your list, but the return can be significant. When I gave my first live webinar, the signups came from people on my list since they already knew me from opting in to my list and through reading my emails that are sent our several times per month.

5. One year! You will need one year to get everything optimized, but this is the quickest path to a successful business. Focusing on the five ones and constantly improving your content is the easiest way to succeed. I have used that principal since starting on this journey and it has made all the difference as I have updated my webinar multiple times and other parts of the program and webinar.

When I learned about the five ones it was an eye opener. The results have been lifechanging and I have learned to live by the five ones ever since.

Ask yourself the following questions:

Do you focus on too many things at once?

Is it time for you to make a change in your life?

Are you willing to use the five ones to be successful?

Chapter 10 Work Hard AND Work Smart

"The dictionary is the only place that success comes before work. Work is the key to success, and hard work can help you accomplish anything." Vince Lombardi

The most important lesson that I have learned over the years is to have a strong work ethic. In June 2015, when I started my own author journey by writing my first book, it was hard work. At that time, I was still teaching and had June and July off. I spent those two months learning everything I could about book publishing and wrote both Eat Less and Move More and Motivation 101.

I was working ten to twelve hours a day and I loved it. When I returned to teaching I had to not only continue to work hard, but also work smart. For the next two years my work week with teaching and running both BrodieEDU and Brodie Consulting Group was at least eighty hours a week.

Becoming an entrepreneur involves working harder than you ever have done before, especially when you are still working full time. I learned to manage literally every minute of my day and wrote eight bestselling books while I was still teaching and coaching multiple clients one-on-one.

The easiest way to succeed in life is to not only outwork everyone else, but to also work smart. Both working hard AND working smart are critical to success. Plan your day into sections. When I am working on my books I would work for periods of sixty to ninety minutes and then make myself take a fifteen to twenty-minute break. It was difficult, but taking a break helped me without avoiding both burnout and writers block.

With leaving teaching and running both businesses, my workweek is back at eighty hours, but it is with not only writing the books, but also coaching the students in my Book Publishing for Authors Implementation Program, creating new webinar and course content, and updating and presenting my motivational seminars.

It is hard work and planning is essential. I recently made a change and now work three blocks a day. In the morning, I will work for fifty minutes straight as part of my quarter hour plus power hour and do the same fifty-minute block both in the afternoon and evening. It was tough at first, but I learned to work more efficiently.

Another thing I did was turn off the wi-fi on my laptop when writing and creating content. It was lifechanging as I would not receive alerts from email or Facebook and it increased my focus dramatically.

It helped cut out the static and made a huge difference. I also turned off my phone during those work times and it increased my productivity significantly

There are still nights, especially during book launches where I might work until midnight, but those days are much less than in the past. In October, I had to get multiple weeks of work done in two weeks prior to leaving for Maui with my Book Publishing for Authors book.

Items included recording the audiobook, which was over twenty-eight thousand words. I recorded and narrated it myself and the final recording was over three hours and forty minutes that was recorded over three days with roughly six hours of time in my home office/recording studio.

I also had to send the final draft to my editor, convert the final draft to paperback format after getting the edits back, get the book cover designs sent to my designer, and send out the final edited draft to my Kindle formatter. There were lots of other moving parts involved and it was hard work getting everything done. I also had to set up the marketing plan and get all the book promos booked. Everything was finalized prior to the trip and I launched the book in Maui to great success and was very proud when it became my tenth bestselling book.

Overall, I was very proud of what was accomplished and you must have the yes mentality and get everything that must be done completed. Work ethic is what will separate you from others and it is the best way to become successful. Again, you must work hard AND work smart to be successful.

In between I was also flying to Myrtle Beach and ended up finalizing the updates to my Motivation 101 seminar on the two flights I had to help maximize my time. Again, running your businesses is hard work, but there is nothing more rewarding then having the freedom to work for yourself, be your own boss, and set your own hours. Having the freedom to travel anywhere in the world whenever you want is an incredibly liberating feeling.

Writing this book while in Maui has been a pleasure as I wanted to share my journey and how it can help you on your journey to develop a successful mindset to become your greatest champion.

Ask yourself the following questions:

Are you willing to work harder than you ever have before to change your life?

Do you work hard or work smart?

Summary: The Journey of a Champion

"We have the ability to be our greatest champion or worst enemy by how we think about our lives each day." Paul Brodie

We have covered a lot of information in this book. There are many moving parts when it comes to developing a successful mindset.

Throughout the book we have covered: ways to develop a successful mindset and becoming your greatest champion by dealing with adversity, making the choice to change your life, why it is important to be coachable, the importance of both gratitude and humility, being all in when it is time to make a potential life-changing choice, the importance of travel in your life, having an accountability partner, why it is important to expand your mind with reading, using the five ones to build a successful business, and having a strong work ethic and working smart.

One thing I want to make clear is that no one can do it themselves. We all need help! I am a huge believer in having help and I hired a business coach earlier this year myself. It was the best decision I ever made with hiring my coach and going through his program. The money I invested in the program was significant, but I have already made significant revenue due to what I learned in his program. It was life changing when I decided to hire a coach to help me implement. Best part is that the investment often is tax deductible. Check with your country's tax laws, but I was able to write off the investment of hiring my own coach on my taxes.

After graduating from the initial program, I met with my coach at his workshop in Santa Monica, California in early October. We spoke about the future and I applied to join his mastermind program called Black Belt. It was a significant investment and the membership was twenty thousand dollars for the next year. After having a follow-up call I was invited to join Black Belt and I accepted. I mention this because having the right mentality is key when you are ready to make serious changes and improvement in your life. The main thing to look for is what will the outcome be? I already know that my outcome with the return on investment will be significant because of the focus, accountability, and implementation that comes with Taki's Black Belt program.

Having a coach brings focus, accountability, and implementation to getting your business built correctly. It also will help build your business quickly with a proven system that works. Whether you are building a business or looking to write and publish your book, I can tell you the hardest part is the implementation process, which is the primary benefit you will get should we end up working together.

One of the most important questions that you need to ask yourself is this.

What are you willing to invest to change your life?

If you are reading this book then you are most likely at a fork in the road. You want to make a change.

The change you want to make involves either expanding your business or starting a new business. If you are a business owner, having a book is essential to build and expand your business. It also most likely involves the goal to leave your current job eventually, especially if you are working for someone else. I know that because that is the situation for most of my clients, and student authors in my Book Publishing for Authors Implementation Program, which offers the ideal system if you are wanting to write, publish and market your book to a #1 bestseller.

I was also in that same situation two years ago when I wrote, published, and marketed my first book. At that time, I was making good money teaching, but I was not making a lot of additional income. After that trip to Las Vegas I started to write my first book. Once the book was written, I realized that I needed more money to be able to pay for my first launch while waiting for the royalties to come in. Once your book is launched, it takes two months to get your first royalty check from Amazon.

I knew that I would be spending at least a couple thousand dollars with publishing and marketing my first book. Once I realized the investment that was necessary, I made the decision to ask my dad for a loan. I told him my business plan and he lent me two thousand dollars so I could get the book published and marketed properly.

That loan resulted in starting a business that now makes significant revenue two years later with multiple revenue streams on the front-end with each of my books releases in Kindle, audiobook, and paperback and on the back-end with speaking events, limited One-On-One coaching, Done for

You publishing and marketing packages, and my primary focus by using the five ones, which is the Book Publishing for Authors Implementation Program.

Taking that risk two years ago and taking the plunge enabled me to leave my job as a teacher, be my own boss, and set my own hours. The commute is now ten seconds from the living room to my home office and I love it. The best part is working with others to help them write, publish and market their books to a #1 bestseller and more importantly helping them change their lives.

Every one of my clients has become a bestseller and I take a lot of pride in that. I strongly recommend investing your time by reading this book and watching your complementary Get Published Online Workshop, which is available at the end of this chapter.

I would love to work with you either through having you join the Book Publishing for Authors Implementation Program, limited One-On-One Coaching, or by publishing and marketing your book for you.

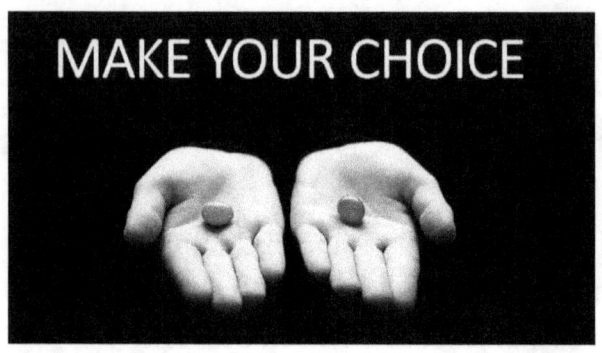

Now it is time for you to decide and answer the following question one more time.

<u>What are you willing to invest to change your life?</u>

Please spread the word about this book and the implementation program with your friends if they are also looking to change their lives. If there is anything I can do for you then please let me know.

Thank you for investing your time in reading my book and I look forward to hearing about your future success.

Go to www.BrodieEDU.com and click on the Free Webinar tab to watch your complementary Get Published Training

Champion Seminar Invitation

I want to invite you to help bring me to your organization or campus event. Each of the self-help books (<u>Motivation 101</u>, <u>Positivity Attracts</u>, <u>The Pursuit of Happiness</u>, <u>PMA</u>, <u>Just Do It</u>, and <u>Champion</u>) that I have published are based on my motivational seminars.

These motivation seminars are interactive and enjoyable for all attendees, while also providing invaluable information to employees, students, faculty, and staff of universities.
The intention of the seminars is to help the audience become their greatest champion by developing a successful mindset, improve motivation, increase positive thinking and

happiness, develop leadership skills, show entrepreneurs how to build a successful business, and help the audience on the journey to achieving their dreams and goals.

Contact me at Brodie@BrodieConsultingGroup.com with any questions.

Go to www.BrodieEDU.com/seminars to see a brief video and to get more information on how to bring Paul to your organization or campus

More Books by Paul

"Quick and inexpensive reads for self-improvement, a healthier lifestyle, and book publishing"

Ten-time Amazon bestselling author, Paul Brodie believes that books should be inexpensive, straightforward, direct, and not have a bunch of fluff.

Each of his books were created to solve problems including living a healthy lifestyle, increasing motivation, improving positive thinking, traveling to amazing destinations, and helping authors write, publish and market their books to a #1 bestseller.

What makes Paul's books different is his ability to explain complex ideas and strategies in a simple, accessible way that you can implement immediately.

Want to know more?

Go to www.BrodieEDU.com/Books

About the Author

Paul Brodie is the President of BrodieEDU, an education consulting firm that specializes in giving motivational, business, publishing, and leadership seminars for universities and corporations. He is also the CEO of Brodie Consulting Group, which specializes in book publishing and coaching clients on how to publish and market their books.

Brodie recently left teaching after serving as an educator in multiple roles since 2008. He served as a Special Education Teacher from 2014-2017 in the Hurst-Euless-Bedford ISD (2014-2016) and Fort Worth ISD (2016-2017) while working specifically with special needs children who had Autism. In 2014-2015 he also served as the head tennis coach and lead the school to a district championship and an undefeated season.

From 2011-2014, Brodie served as a Grant Coordinator for the ASPIRE program in the Birdville Independent School District. As coordinator, he created instructional and enrichment programming for over 800 students and 100 parents in the ASPIRE before and after school programs. He also served on the Board of Directors for the Leadership Development Council, Inc. from 2005-2014 with leading the implementation of educational programming in low cost housing.

From 2008-2011, he was a highly successful teacher in Arlington, TX where he taught English as a Second Language. Brodie turned a once struggling ESL program into one of the top programs in the school district. Many of his students moved on to journalism, AVID, art classes, and many students exited the ESL program entirely.

Teaching methods during his career as an educator included daily writing practice, flash cards, picture cards, academic relays, music, movies, and short educational videos including the alphabet and sight words. Additional strategies included graphic novels paired with movie versions of the novels, games, cultural celebrations, and getting parents involved in their children's education. Brodie's approach has been called unconventional but very effective, revolutionary, and highly engaging. His students have always shown great improvement with both academics and behavior throughout the school year and he was honored to teach such an amazing and diverse group of students during his career as an educator.

Previously, Brodie spent many years in the corporate world and decided to leave a lucrative career in the medical field to follow his passion and transitioned into education. Prior to working in the medical field, he worked for Enterprise Rent-A-Car after receiving his Bachelor's Degree and for Savitz Research during his high school and college years. He is very grateful for every career opportunity as each one was an avenue to learn and grow.

Brodie earned an M.A. in Teaching from Louisiana College and B.B.A. in Management from the University of Texas at Arlington. Brodie is a bestselling author and has written multiple books. He wrote his first book, Eat Less and Move More: My Journey in the summer of 2015. Brodie's goal of the book was to help those like himself who had challenges with weight. The goal of his first book was to promote not only weight loss but also health and wellness. He is also the author of Motivation 101, Positivity Attracts, Book Publishing for Beginners, The Pursuit of Happiness, Maui, Just Do It, PMA, San Diego and Book Publishing for Authors. All ten books (available in Kindle, Paperback, and Audiobook) are Amazon bestsellers and are based on his motivational seminars, book publishing, love of travel, and struggles with weight.

His seminars have been featured at many universities and at leadership conferences across the United States since 2005. Brodie is active in professional organizations and within the community and currently serves on the Advisory Board for Advent Urban Youth Development and as a volunteer with the Special Olympics. He continues to be involved with The International Business Fraternity of Delta Sigma Pi and has served in many positions since 2002 including National Vice President – Organizational Development, Leadership Foundation Trustee, National Organizational Development Chair, District Director, and in many other volunteer leadership roles. He resides in Arlington, TX.

Acknowledgments

Thank you to God for guidance and protection throughout my life.

Thank YOU, the reader, for investing your time reading this book.

Thank you to my amazing mom, Barbara Brodie for all the years of support and a kick in the butt when needed.

Thank you to my awesome sister, Dr. Heather Ottaway for all the help and feedback with my books and with my motivational seminars. It is scary how similar we are.

Thank you to Devin Mooneyham for serving as the editor of my eleventh book. The slicing and dicing as always was very much appreciated and I could not have gotten this book published without her assistance.

Thank you to Lindsay Palmer who is working tirelessly to get me booked on college campuses for seminars throughout the United States. I could not have a better team of people to work with on Team Brodie.

Thank you to all who have served on the BrodieEDU Advisory Board.

Thank you to my dad, Bill "The Wild Scotsman" Brodie for his encouragement and support with the business aspects of BrodieEDU and Brodie Consulting Group.

Thank you to Shannon and Robert Winckel (two members of the four horsemen with myself and our good friend, Derrada Rubell-Asbell) for their friendship and support. Shannon and Robert are two of my best teacher friends and are always great sounding boards for ideas.

Thank you to (Don) Omar Sandoval for his friendship and help with several BrodieEDU projects including building our awesome website.

Thank you to all the amazing friends that I have worked with over the past twenty plus years. Each of them has made a great impact on my life.

Thank you to all my students that I have had the honor to teach over the years. I am very proud of each of my kids.

Thank you to Delta Sigma Pi Business Fraternity. I learned a great deal about public speaking and leadership through the organization and every experience that I have had helped me become the person that I am today.

Thank you to my three best friends: J. Dean Craig, Jen Mamber, and Aaron Krzycki. We have gone through a lot together and I look forward to many more years of friendship.

Thank you to my dear friends Schreese Fontaine and Symeon Melikoglou for your many years of friendship. You two are family to me and always will be.

Thank you to all the students past and present at the UT Arlington and UT Austin chapters of DSP. Both schools mean a lot to me and I look forward to seeing them again at some point soon.

Thank you to the Lott Family (Stacy, Kerry, Lexi, and Austin) for their friendship over the past seven years.

Thank you to Robin Clites for always taking care of things at the house with ensuring that Mom and I can always get those family vacations every year.

Contact Information

Go to www.BrodieEDU.com/seminars to see why you should consider booking Paul for your campus or organization.

Paul can be reached at Brodie@BrodieConsultingGroup.com

Website www.BrodieEDU.com

@BrodieEDU on Twitter

Paul G. Brodie author page on Facebook

Paul G. Brodie author page on Amazon

BrodieEDU Facebook Page

BrodieEDU YouTube Channel

Quotes

I wanted to share with you the quotes that I used to start each chapter of Champion.

Enjoy,

Paul

Chapter 1 Dealing with Adversity

"Everybody has a plan until they get hit in the face." Mike Tyson

Chapter 2 Make a Choice

"I guess it comes down to a simple choice: Get busy living, or get busy dying." Andy Dufresne (as played by Tim Robbins in the Shawshank Redemption)

Chapter 3 Be Coachable

"The journey of a thousand miles begins with one step." Lao Tzu

Chapter 4 Gratitude and Humility

"Gratitude is the healthiest of all human emotions. The more you express gratitude for what you have, the more likely you will have even more to express gratitude for." Zig Ziglar

Chapter 5 Going All In

"Life, like poker has an element of risk. It shouldn't be avoided. It should be faced." Edward Norton

Chapter 6 Travel

"To travel is to take a journey into yourself." Danny Kaye

Chapter 7 Having an Accountability Partner

"Great leaders understand that talented people thrive in a culture where accountability is a support system for success." Daniel Pink

Chapter 8 Expand Your Mind

"I fear not the man who has practiced 10,000 kicks once, but I fear the man who had practiced one kick 10,000 times." Bruce Lee

Chapter 9 The Five Ones

"It is those who concentrate on but one thing at a time who advance in this world." Gary Keller

Chapter 10 Work Ethic

"The dictionary is the only place that success comes before work. Work is the key to success, and hard work can help you accomplish anything." Vince Lombardi

Summary: The Journey of a Champion

"We have the ability to be our greatest champion or worst enemy by how we think about our lives each day." Paul Brodie

Feedback

Please leave a review for my book as I would greatly appreciate your feedback.

I also welcome you to contact me with any suggestions at Brodie@BrodieConsultingGroup.com

www.ingramcontent.com/pod-product-compliance
Lightning Source LLC
Chambersburg PA
CBHW050231230526
45470CB00005B/1901